50 Iranian Kebab and Rice Recipes for Home

By: Kelly Johnson

Table of Contents

- Joojeh Kebab (Grilled Chicken Kebab)
- Kubideh Kebab (Ground Meat Kebab)
- Barg Kebab (Filet Mignon Kebab)
- Chelo Kebab (Rice with Kebab)
- Soltani Kebab (Combination of Kubideh and Barg)
- Koobideh Morgh (Ground Chicken Kebab)
- Chenjeh Kebab (Lamb Shoulder Kebab)
- Mahi Kebab (Grilled Fish Kebab)
- Shahi Kebab (Royal Kebab)
- Kebab Torsh (Sour Kebab)
- Kebab Tabeh (Grilled Tomato Kebab)
- Kebab Bakhtiari (Combination of Kubideh and Joojeh)
- Adana Kebab (Spicy Ground Meat Kebab)
- Chapli Kebab (Pakistani Style Meat Kebab)
- Tavuk Şiş (Turkish Chicken Kebab)
- Shish Kebab (Classic Skewered Meat)
- Koobideh Barg (Ground Beef Fillet Kebab)
- Koobideh Saffron (Saffron-infused Ground Meat Kebab)
- Persian Rice with Saffron Kebab
- Baghali Polo with Lamb Kebab (Rice with Fava Beans and Lamb Kebab)
- Zereshk Polo with Chicken Kebab (Barberry Rice with Chicken Kebab)
- Albaloo Polo with Beef Kebab (Sour Cherry Rice with Beef Kebab)
- Lubia Polo with Joojeh Kebab (Green Bean Rice with Grilled Chicken)
- Shirin Polo with Kubideh Kebab (Sweet Rice with Ground Meat Kebab)
- Adas Polo with Barg Kebab (Lentil Rice with Filet Mignon Kebab)
- Kebab-e Masti (Creamy Kebab)
- Kebab Kubideh (Ground Beef Kebab)
- Jigar Kebab (Liver Kebab)
- Kebab Tabei (Pan-Fried Kebab)
- Kebab-e Torki (Turkish Kebab)
- Kebab-e Morgh (Chicken Kebab)
- Gheymeh Kebab (Split Pea Stew with Kebab)
- Bademjan Kebab (Eggplant and Meat Kebab)
- Baghali Polo with Joojeh Kebab (Rice with Dill and Grilled Chicken)
- Kebab-e Torsh (Sour Kebab)

- Zaban Kebab (Tongue Kebab)
- Kebab-e Nokhodchi (Chickpea Kebab)
- Kebab-e Lari (Lari Kebab)
- Kebab-e Borani (Borani Kebab)
- Kebab-e Dandeh (Sheep Kebab)
- Kebab-e Shalgham
- Kebab-e Jigar (Liver Kebab)
- Kebab-e Falafel (Falafel Kebab)
- Kebab-e Khashkhash (Poppy Seed Kebab)
- Kebab-e Mast (Yogurt Kebab)
- Kebab-e Jujeh (Cornish Hen Kebab)
- Kebab-e Sabzi (Herb Kebab)
- Kebab-e Taze (Fresh Kebab)
- Kebab-e Shirazi (Shirazi Kebab)
- Kebab-e Esfenaj (Spinach Kebab)

Joojeh Kebab (Grilled Chicken Kebab)

Ingredients:

- 4 boneless, skinless chicken breasts or thighs
- 1 large onion, grated
- 3 cloves garlic, minced
- 1/4 cup plain yogurt
- Juice of 1 lemon
- 2 tablespoons olive oil
- 1 teaspoon ground saffron (dissolved in 2 tablespoons hot water)
- 1 teaspoon ground turmeric
- 1 teaspoon ground black pepper
- 1 teaspoon salt, or to taste
- Wooden skewers, soaked in water for at least 30 minutes

Instructions:

1. Cut the chicken breasts or thighs into bite-sized pieces and place them in a large bowl.
2. In a separate bowl, combine the grated onion, minced garlic, yogurt, lemon juice, olive oil, saffron water, turmeric, black pepper, and salt. Mix well to combine.
3. Pour the marinade over the chicken pieces, making sure they are evenly coated. Cover the bowl with plastic wrap and refrigerate for at least 2 hours, or preferably overnight, to allow the flavors to meld.
4. Preheat your grill to medium-high heat. If using charcoal, wait until the coals are ashed over.
5. Thread the marinated chicken pieces onto the soaked wooden skewers, leaving a little space between each piece.
6. Brush the grill grates lightly with oil to prevent sticking. Place the skewers on the grill and cook for 6-8 minutes per side, or until the chicken is cooked through and has nice grill marks.
7. Once cooked, remove the skewers from the grill and let them rest for a few minutes before serving.
8. Serve the Joojeh Kebab hot with rice, grilled vegetables, and a squeeze of lemon juice if desired.

Enjoy your homemade Joojeh Kebab!

Kubideh Kebab (Ground Meat Kebab)

Ingredients:

- 1 pound ground beef or lamb (or a combination of both)
- 1 onion, grated
- 2 cloves garlic, minced
- 1 egg
- 1 teaspoon ground turmeric
- 1 teaspoon ground sumac (optional)
- 1 teaspoon ground cumin
- 1 teaspoon ground coriander
- 1 teaspoon salt, or to taste
- 1/2 teaspoon black pepper
- 1/4 cup chopped fresh parsley (optional)
- Wooden skewers, soaked in water for at least 30 minutes

Instructions:

1. In a large mixing bowl, combine the ground meat, grated onion, minced garlic, egg, turmeric, sumac (if using), cumin, coriander, salt, black pepper, and chopped parsley (if using). Mix well until all the ingredients are evenly incorporated.
2. Divide the meat mixture into equal portions and shape each portion into a long, cylindrical sausage shape, about 1 inch in diameter.
3. Preheat your grill to medium-high heat. If using charcoal, wait until the coals are ashed over.
4. Thread the meat onto the soaked wooden skewers, pressing and shaping the meat gently to form a long, even kebab.
5. Brush the grill grates lightly with oil to prevent sticking. Place the skewers on the grill and cook for 4-5 minutes per side, or until the meat is cooked through and has nice grill marks.
6. Once cooked, remove the skewers from the grill and let them rest for a few minutes before serving.
7. Serve the Kubideh Kebab hot with rice, flatbread, grilled vegetables, and a squeeze of lemon juice if desired.

Enjoy your homemade Kubideh Kebab!

Barg Kebab (Filet Mignon Kebab)

Ingredients:

- 1 pound filet mignon, cut into thin slices
- 1 onion, grated
- 4 cloves garlic, minced
- 1/4 cup plain yogurt
- Juice of 1 lemon
- 2 tablespoons olive oil
- 1 teaspoon ground saffron (dissolved in 2 tablespoons hot water)
- 1 teaspoon ground turmeric
- 1 teaspoon ground black pepper
- 1 teaspoon salt, or to taste
- Wooden skewers, soaked in water for at least 30 minutes

Instructions:

1. In a large mixing bowl, combine the grated onion, minced garlic, yogurt, lemon juice, olive oil, saffron water, turmeric, black pepper, and salt. Mix well to combine.
2. Add the thinly sliced filet mignon to the marinade, making sure each slice is coated evenly. Cover the bowl with plastic wrap and refrigerate for at least 2 hours, or preferably overnight, to allow the flavors to meld.
3. Preheat your grill to medium-high heat. If using charcoal, wait until the coals are ashed over.
4. Thread the marinated filet mignon slices onto the soaked wooden skewers, weaving them onto the skewers to create an even layer.
5. Brush the grill grates lightly with oil to prevent sticking. Place the skewers on the grill and cook for 2-3 minutes per side, or until the meat is cooked to your desired level of doneness.
6. Once cooked, remove the skewers from the grill and let them rest for a few minutes before serving.
7. Serve the Barg Kebab hot with rice, flatbread, grilled vegetables, and a squeeze of lemon juice if desired.

Enjoy your homemade Barg Kebab, with its tender and flavorful filet mignon slices!

Chelo Kebab (Rice with Kebab)

Ingredients for Chelo (Steamed Saffron Rice):

- 2 cups basmati rice
- 4 cups water
- 2 tablespoons butter or ghee
- 1 teaspoon salt
- Pinch of saffron threads
- 2 tablespoons hot water

Ingredients for Kebab (choose your favorite kebab variety, such as Kubideh, Joojeh, or Barg):

- Kebab of your choice (enough for serving)
- Skewers (if needed)
- Olive oil (for grilling)
- Salt and pepper (for seasoning, if needed)

Instructions for Chelo (Steamed Saffron Rice):

1. Rinse the basmati rice under cold water until the water runs clear. Drain well.
2. In a large pot, bring 4 cups of water to a boil. Add the rinsed and drained rice to the boiling water.
3. Cook the rice uncovered on medium-high heat for about 6-8 minutes or until it's parboiled. Stir occasionally.
4. Drain the parboiled rice in a fine-mesh sieve and rinse it quickly with cold water to stop the cooking process.
5. In a small bowl, dissolve a pinch of saffron threads in 2 tablespoons of hot water. Let it steep for a few minutes.
6. In a large non-stick pot, melt the butter or ghee over low heat. Once melted, add a layer of rice to the bottom of the pot.
7. Drizzle some of the saffron water over the rice layer. Repeat layering the rice and saffron water until all the rice is used. Sprinkle salt over the top layer.
8. Cover the pot with a tight-fitting lid wrapped in a clean kitchen towel or foil to trap the steam. Cook the rice over low heat for about 30-40 minutes, or until the rice is fluffy and fully cooked.

Instructions for Kebab:

1. Prepare your favorite kebab variety according to the specific recipe instructions. If using skewers, thread the meat onto the skewers.
2. Preheat your grill to medium-high heat. If using charcoal, wait until the coals are ashed over.
3. Brush the grill grates lightly with olive oil to prevent sticking.
4. Place the kebabs on the grill and cook them according to the recipe instructions or until they are fully cooked and have grill marks on all sides.
5. Season the kebabs with salt and pepper, if needed, while grilling.

Assembly:

1. Once the rice and kebabs are ready, serve the Chelo Kebab hot. Place a mound of steamed saffron rice on each plate.
2. Arrange the grilled kebabs on top of the rice.
3. Garnish with additional saffron threads or chopped fresh herbs, if desired.
4. Serve with grilled tomatoes, onions, and flatbread on the side, along with yogurt or salad.

Enjoy your homemade Chelo Kebab, a delicious and comforting Iranian dish!

Soltani Kebab (Combination of Kubideh and Barg)

Ingredients:

For Kubideh (Ground Meat Kebab):

- 1 pound ground beef or lamb (or a combination of both)
- 1 onion, grated
- 2 cloves garlic, minced
- 1 egg
- 1 teaspoon ground turmeric
- 1 teaspoon ground sumac (optional)
- 1 teaspoon ground cumin
- 1 teaspoon ground coriander
- 1 teaspoon salt, or to taste
- 1/2 teaspoon black pepper
- 1/4 cup chopped fresh parsley (optional)

For Barg (Filet Mignon Kebab):

- 1 pound filet mignon, cut into thin slices
- 1 onion, grated
- 4 cloves garlic, minced
- 1/4 cup plain yogurt
- Juice of 1 lemon
- 2 tablespoons olive oil
- 1 teaspoon ground saffron (dissolved in 2 tablespoons hot water)
- 1 teaspoon ground turmeric
- 1 teaspoon ground black pepper
- 1 teaspoon salt, or to taste

For Serving:

- Steamed saffron rice (Chelo)
- Grilled tomatoes and onions
- Flatbread (such as Lavash or Pita)
- Yogurt or salad for serving

Instructions:

For Kubideh (Ground Meat Kebab):

1. In a large mixing bowl, combine the ground meat, grated onion, minced garlic, egg, turmeric, sumac (if using), cumin, coriander, salt, black pepper, and chopped parsley (if using). Mix well until all the ingredients are evenly incorporated.
2. Divide the meat mixture into equal portions and shape each portion into a long, cylindrical sausage shape, about 1 inch in diameter.
3. Preheat your grill to medium-high heat. If using charcoal, wait until the coals are ashed over.
4. Thread the meat onto skewers, shaping them gently to form an even layer.
5. Brush the grill grates lightly with oil to prevent sticking. Place the skewers on the grill and cook for 4-5 minutes per side, or until the meat is cooked through and has nice grill marks.

For Barg (Filet Mignon Kebab):

1. In a large mixing bowl, combine the grated onion, minced garlic, yogurt, lemon juice, olive oil, saffron water, turmeric, black pepper, and salt. Mix well to combine.
2. Add the thinly sliced filet mignon to the marinade, making sure each slice is coated evenly. Cover the bowl with plastic wrap and refrigerate for at least 2 hours, or preferably overnight, to allow the flavors to meld.
3. Preheat your grill to medium-high heat. If using charcoal, wait until the coals are ashed over.
4. Thread the marinated filet mignon slices onto skewers.
5. Brush the grill grates lightly with oil to prevent sticking. Place the skewers on the grill and cook for 2-3 minutes per side, or until the meat is cooked to your desired level of doneness.

For Serving:

1. Once both types of kebabs are cooked, remove them from the grill and arrange them on a serving platter.
2. Serve the Soltani Kebab hot with steamed saffron rice (Chelo), grilled tomatoes and onions, and flatbread.
3. Accompany with yogurt or salad on the side.

Enjoy your homemade Soltani Kebab, a delicious combination of flavors and textures!

Koobideh Morgh (Ground Chicken Kebab)

Ingredients:

- 1 pound ground chicken
- 1 small onion, grated
- 2 cloves garlic, minced
- 1 tablespoon fresh lime juice
- 2 tablespoons plain yogurt
- 1 teaspoon ground turmeric
- 1 teaspoon ground sumac (optional)
- 1 teaspoon ground cumin
- 1 teaspoon ground coriander
- 1 teaspoon salt, or to taste
- 1/2 teaspoon black pepper
- 1/4 cup chopped fresh parsley or cilantro (optional)
- Wooden skewers, soaked in water for at least 30 minutes

Instructions:

1. In a large mixing bowl, combine the ground chicken, grated onion, minced garlic, lime juice, yogurt, turmeric, sumac (if using), cumin, coriander, salt, black pepper, and chopped parsley or cilantro (if using). Mix well until all the ingredients are evenly incorporated.
2. Cover the bowl with plastic wrap and refrigerate for at least 1 hour to allow the flavors to meld.
3. Preheat your grill to medium-high heat. If using charcoal, wait until the coals are ashed over.
4. Divide the chicken mixture into equal portions. Take one portion and shape it into a long, cylindrical sausage shape, about 1 inch in diameter, around a wooden skewer. Repeat with the remaining portions.
5. Brush the grill grates lightly with oil to prevent sticking. Place the skewers on the grill and cook for 5-6 minutes per side, or until the chicken is cooked through and has nice grill marks.
6. Once cooked, remove the skewers from the grill and let them rest for a few minutes before serving.
7. Serve the Koobideh Morgh hot with rice, flatbread, grilled vegetables, and a squeeze of lime juice if desired.

Enjoy your homemade Koobideh Morgh, a delicious and healthy alternative to traditional kebabs!

Chenjeh Kebab (Lamb Shoulder Kebab)

Ingredients:

- 1.5 pounds lamb shoulder, cut into 1-inch cubes
- 1 onion, grated
- 3 cloves garlic, minced
- 1/4 cup plain yogurt
- Juice of 1 lemon
- 2 tablespoons olive oil
- 1 teaspoon ground saffron (dissolved in 2 tablespoons hot water)
- 1 teaspoon ground turmeric
- 1 teaspoon ground black pepper
- 1 teaspoon salt, or to taste
- 1/4 cup chopped fresh parsley or cilantro (optional)
- Wooden skewers, soaked in water for at least 30 minutes

Instructions:

1. In a large mixing bowl, combine the grated onion, minced garlic, yogurt, lemon juice, olive oil, saffron water, turmeric, black pepper, salt, and chopped parsley or cilantro (if using). Mix well to combine.
2. Add the lamb shoulder cubes to the marinade, ensuring each piece is coated evenly. Cover the bowl with plastic wrap and refrigerate for at least 2 hours, or preferably overnight, to allow the flavors to meld.
3. Preheat your grill to medium-high heat. If using charcoal, wait until the coals are ashed over.
4. Thread the marinated lamb shoulder cubes onto the soaked wooden skewers, leaving a little space between each piece.
5. Brush the grill grates lightly with oil to prevent sticking. Place the skewers on the grill and cook for 5-6 minutes per side, or until the lamb is cooked through and has a nice char on the outside.
6. Once cooked, remove the skewers from the grill and let them rest for a few minutes before serving.
7. Serve the Chenjeh Kebab hot with rice, flatbread, grilled vegetables, and a squeeze of lemon juice if desired.

Enjoy your homemade Chenjeh Kebab, featuring tender and flavorful lamb shoulder cubes!

Mahi Kebab (Grilled Fish Kebab)

Ingredients:

- 1 pound firm-fleshed fish fillets (such as salmon, tuna, or swordfish), cut into 1-inch cubes
- 1 onion, grated
- 3 cloves garlic, minced
- Juice of 1 lemon
- 2 tablespoons olive oil
- 1 teaspoon ground saffron (dissolved in 2 tablespoons hot water)
- 1 teaspoon ground turmeric
- 1 teaspoon ground cumin
- 1 teaspoon ground coriander
- 1 teaspoon salt, or to taste
- 1/2 teaspoon black pepper
- Wooden skewers, soaked in water for at least 30 minutes

Instructions:

1. In a large mixing bowl, combine the grated onion, minced garlic, lemon juice, olive oil, saffron water, turmeric, cumin, coriander, salt, and black pepper. Mix well to combine.
2. Add the fish cubes to the marinade, ensuring each piece is coated evenly. Cover the bowl with plastic wrap and refrigerate for at least 30 minutes to marinate.
3. Preheat your grill to medium-high heat. If using charcoal, wait until the coals are ashed over.
4. Thread the marinated fish cubes onto the soaked wooden skewers, leaving a little space between each piece.
5. Brush the grill grates lightly with oil to prevent sticking. Place the skewers on the grill and cook for 3-4 minutes per side, or until the fish is cooked through and has nice grill marks.
6. Once cooked, remove the skewers from the grill and let them rest for a few minutes before serving.
7. Serve the Mahi Kebab hot with rice, flatbread, grilled vegetables, and a squeeze of lemon juice if desired.

Enjoy your homemade Mahi Kebab, featuring tender and flavorful grilled fish!

Shahi Kebab (Royal Kebab)

Ingredients:

For the Marinade:

- 1 pound boneless meat (such as lamb, beef, or chicken), cut into bite-sized pieces
- 1 cup plain yogurt
- 1 tablespoon ginger paste
- 1 tablespoon garlic paste
- 1 teaspoon ground turmeric
- 1 teaspoon ground cumin
- 1 teaspoon ground coriander
- 1 teaspoon ground cardamom
- 1 teaspoon garam masala
- 1 teaspoon paprika or Kashmiri red chili powder
- 1 teaspoon salt, or to taste
- Juice of 1 lemon
- 2 tablespoons vegetable oil

For the Gravy:

- 2 tablespoons ghee or vegetable oil
- 1 large onion, finely chopped
- 2 tomatoes, finely chopped
- 1 tablespoon ginger paste
- 1 tablespoon garlic paste
- 1 teaspoon ground turmeric
- 1 teaspoon ground cumin
- 1 teaspoon ground coriander
- 1 teaspoon garam masala
- 1/2 cup heavy cream
- Salt and pepper to taste
- Chopped fresh cilantro or mint for garnish

Instructions:

1. In a large bowl, combine the yogurt, ginger paste, garlic paste, turmeric, cumin, coriander, cardamom, garam masala, paprika or chili powder, salt, lemon juice, and vegetable oil to make the marinade. Mix well.
2. Add the bite-sized meat pieces to the marinade and coat them evenly. Cover the bowl and let the meat marinate in the refrigerator for at least 2 hours, or overnight for best results.
3. Preheat your grill to medium-high heat. If using charcoal, wait until the coals are ashed over.
4. Thread the marinated meat pieces onto skewers, leaving a little space between each piece.
5. Brush the grill grates lightly with oil to prevent sticking. Place the skewers on the grill and cook for 8-10 minutes, turning occasionally, until the meat is cooked through and has a nice char.
6. While the meat is grilling, prepare the gravy. In a large skillet, heat ghee or vegetable oil over medium heat. Add the finely chopped onion and sauté until golden brown.
7. Add the ginger paste and garlic paste to the skillet and sauté for another 2-3 minutes until fragrant.
8. Add the chopped tomatoes to the skillet and cook until they soften and release their juices.
9. Stir in the turmeric, cumin, coriander, and garam masala. Cook for another 2-3 minutes, allowing the spices to toast and become fragrant.
10. Pour in the heavy cream and mix well to combine. Season with salt and pepper to taste.
11. Once the meat is cooked, remove the skewers from the grill and transfer the meat pieces to the skillet with the gravy. Gently toss to coat the meat with the gravy.
12. Garnish the Shahi Kebab with chopped fresh cilantro or mint before serving.
13. Serve hot with rice, naan, or flatbread.

Enjoy your Shahi Kebab, fit for royalty, with its rich and aromatic flavors!

Kebab Torsh (Sour Kebab)

Ingredients:

For the Marinade:

- 1.5 pounds boneless meat (beef, lamb, or chicken), cut into cubes
- 2 onions, grated
- 4 cloves garlic, minced
- 1/2 cup pomegranate molasses
- 1/4 cup olive oil
- Juice of 1 lemon
- 1 tablespoon ground turmeric
- 1 tablespoon ground cinnamon
- 1 teaspoon ground cumin
- 1 teaspoon ground coriander
- Salt and pepper to taste

For the Sauce:

- 2 tablespoons olive oil
- 1 onion, finely chopped
- 1 cup walnuts, finely chopped
- 1/4 cup pomegranate molasses
- 1 cup chicken or beef broth
- 1 tablespoon sugar (optional)
- Salt and pepper to taste

Instructions:

1. In a large mixing bowl, combine the grated onions, minced garlic, pomegranate molasses, olive oil, lemon juice, turmeric, cinnamon, cumin, coriander, salt, and pepper to make the marinade.
2. Add the meat cubes to the marinade and toss until well coated. Cover the bowl and refrigerate for at least 2 hours, or overnight for best results.
3. Preheat your grill to medium-high heat. If using charcoal, wait until the coals are ashed over.

4. Thread the marinated meat cubes onto skewers, leaving a little space between each piece.
5. Brush the grill grates lightly with oil to prevent sticking. Place the skewers on the grill and cook for 8-10 minutes, turning occasionally, until the meat is cooked through and has a nice char.
6. While the meat is grilling, prepare the sauce. Heat olive oil in a skillet over medium heat. Add the finely chopped onion and sauté until softened and translucent.
7. Add the chopped walnuts to the skillet and toast them lightly for 2-3 minutes.
8. Stir in the pomegranate molasses and chicken or beef broth. Bring the mixture to a simmer.
9. If desired, add sugar to balance the tartness of the pomegranate molasses. Season with salt and pepper to taste.
10. Allow the sauce to simmer for 10-15 minutes, or until it thickens slightly.
11. Once the meat is cooked, remove the skewers from the grill and transfer the meat to a serving platter.
12. Pour the prepared sauce over the grilled meat, ensuring it is evenly coated.
13. Garnish the Kebab Torsh with chopped parsley or cilantro before serving.
14. Serve hot with rice or flatbread.

Enjoy the unique and tangy flavor of Kebab Torsh, a delightful Iranian dish that will tantalize your taste buds!

Kebab Tabeh (Grilled Tomato Kebab)

Ingredients:

- 4 large ripe tomatoes
- 2 tablespoons olive oil
- 2 cloves garlic, minced
- 1 teaspoon ground cumin
- 1 teaspoon paprika
- Salt and pepper to taste
- Fresh herbs (such as parsley or cilantro) for garnish

Instructions:

1. Preheat your grill to medium-high heat. If using charcoal, wait until the coals are ashed over.
2. Wash the tomatoes and pat them dry. Slice each tomato into thick slices, about 1/2 inch thick.
3. In a small bowl, whisk together the olive oil, minced garlic, ground cumin, paprika, salt, and pepper to make the marinade.
4. Brush both sides of the tomato slices with the marinade, ensuring they are evenly coated.
5. Place the tomato slices directly on the grill grates. Grill for 3-4 minutes per side, or until the tomatoes are softened and have grill marks.
6. Once the tomatoes are cooked, remove them from the grill and transfer them to a serving platter.
7. Garnish the Kebab Tabeh with fresh herbs, such as parsley or cilantro, before serving.
8. Serve hot as a side dish or appetizer alongside grilled meats or rice dishes.

Enjoy the smoky and savory flavor of Kebab Tabeh, a delightful addition to any meal!

Kebab Bakhtiari (Combination of Kubideh and Joojeh)

Ingredients:

For Kubideh (Ground Meat Kebab):

- 1 pound ground beef or lamb
- 1 onion, grated
- 2 cloves garlic, minced
- 1 teaspoon ground turmeric
- 1 teaspoon ground sumac (optional)
- 1 teaspoon ground cumin
- 1 teaspoon ground coriander
- 1 teaspoon salt, or to taste
- 1/2 teaspoon black pepper
- 1/4 cup chopped fresh parsley (optional)

For Joojeh (Grilled Chicken Kebab):

- 4 boneless, skinless chicken breasts
- 1 onion, grated
- 3 cloves garlic, minced
- 1/4 cup plain yogurt
- Juice of 1 lemon
- 2 tablespoons olive oil
- 1 teaspoon ground saffron (dissolved in 2 tablespoons hot water)
- 1 teaspoon ground turmeric
- 1 teaspoon ground black pepper
- 1 teaspoon salt, or to taste

Instructions:

For Kubideh (Ground Meat Kebab):

1. In a large mixing bowl, combine the ground meat, grated onion, minced garlic, turmeric, sumac (if using), cumin, coriander, salt, black pepper, and chopped parsley (if using). Mix well until all the ingredients are evenly incorporated.

2. Divide the meat mixture into equal portions and shape each portion into a long, cylindrical sausage shape, about 1 inch in diameter.
3. Preheat your grill to medium-high heat. If using charcoal, wait until the coals are ashed over.
4. Thread the meat onto skewers, shaping them gently to form an even layer.
5. Brush the grill grates lightly with oil to prevent sticking. Place the skewers on the grill and cook for 4-5 minutes per side, or until the meat is cooked through and has nice grill marks.

For Joojeh (Grilled Chicken Kebab):

1. In a large mixing bowl, combine the grated onion, minced garlic, yogurt, lemon juice, olive oil, saffron water, turmeric, black pepper, and salt. Mix well to combine.
2. Add the chicken breasts to the marinade, making sure each piece is coated evenly. Cover the bowl with plastic wrap and refrigerate for at least 2 hours, or preferably overnight, to allow the flavors to meld.
3. Preheat your grill to medium-high heat. If using charcoal, wait until the coals are ashed over.
4. Thread the marinated chicken breasts onto skewers.
5. Brush the grill grates lightly with oil to prevent sticking. Place the skewers on the grill and cook for 6-8 minutes per side, or until the chicken is cooked through and has nice grill marks.

Assembly:

1. Once both types of kebabs are cooked, remove them from the grill and transfer them to a serving platter.
2. Serve the Kebab Bakhtiari hot with rice, flatbread, grilled vegetables, and a squeeze of lemon juice if desired.

Enjoy your homemade Kebab Bakhtiari, featuring a delicious combination of ground meat and grilled chicken kebabs!

Adana Kebab (Spicy Ground Meat Kebab)

Ingredients:

- 1 pound ground lamb or beef (or a combination of both)
- 1 onion, grated
- 2 cloves garlic, minced
- 1 tablespoon tomato paste
- 1 tablespoon pepper paste (optional, for extra heat)
- 1 tablespoon paprika
- 1 teaspoon ground cumin
- 1 teaspoon ground coriander
- 1 teaspoon sumac (optional, for tanginess)
- 1 teaspoon red pepper flakes (adjust to taste for desired spiciness)
- Salt and pepper to taste
- Wooden skewers, soaked in water for at least 30 minutes

Instructions:

1. In a large mixing bowl, combine the grated onion, minced garlic, tomato paste, pepper paste (if using), paprika, cumin, coriander, sumac (if using), red pepper flakes, salt, and pepper. Mix well to combine.
2. Add the ground lamb or beef to the spice mixture and mix thoroughly, ensuring that the meat is evenly coated with the spices.
3. Cover the bowl with plastic wrap and refrigerate for at least 1 hour to allow the flavors to meld.
4. Preheat your grill to medium-high heat. If using charcoal, wait until the coals are ashed over.
5. Divide the meat mixture into equal portions. Take one portion and shape it around a wooden skewer, forming a long, cylindrical sausage shape. Repeat with the remaining portions.
6. Brush the grill grates lightly with oil to prevent sticking. Place the skewers on the grill and cook for 4-5 minutes per side, or until the meat is cooked through and has nice grill marks.
7. Once cooked, remove the skewers from the grill and let them rest for a few minutes before serving.
8. Serve the Adana Kebab hot with rice, flatbread, grilled vegetables, and a squeeze of lemon juice if desired.

Enjoy your homemade Adana Kebab, bursting with spicy and savory flavors!

Chapli Kebab (Pakistani Style Meat Kebab)

Ingredients:

- 1 pound ground beef or lamb
- 1 onion, finely chopped
- 2 tomatoes, finely chopped
- 2 green chilies, finely chopped (adjust to taste)
- 1/4 cup fresh cilantro, chopped
- 1/4 cup fresh mint leaves, chopped
- 2 tablespoons ginger paste
- 2 tablespoons garlic paste
- 1 tablespoon ground coriander
- 1 tablespoon ground cumin
- 1 teaspoon ground chili powder (adjust to taste)
- 1 teaspoon ground turmeric
- 1 teaspoon garam masala
- 1 teaspoon salt, or to taste
- 1 egg
- 1/4 cup besan (gram flour/chickpea flour)
- Vegetable oil for frying
- Lemon wedges for serving
- Fresh cilantro leaves for garnish

Instructions:

1. In a large mixing bowl, combine the ground meat, chopped onion, chopped tomatoes, chopped green chilies, chopped cilantro, chopped mint leaves, ginger paste, garlic paste, ground coriander, ground cumin, chili powder, turmeric, garam masala, salt, egg, and besan (gram flour). Mix well until all ingredients are thoroughly combined.
2. Divide the mixture into equal portions and shape each portion into a flat patty, about 1/2 inch thick.
3. Heat vegetable oil in a large skillet over medium heat.
4. Once the oil is hot, carefully place the chapli kebabs in the skillet. Cook for 4-5 minutes on each side, or until they are golden brown and cooked through.
5. Remove the chapli kebabs from the skillet and drain on paper towels to remove excess oil.

6. Serve the chapli kebabs hot with lemon wedges on the side for squeezing over the kebabs.
7. Garnish with fresh cilantro leaves before serving.

Enjoy your homemade Chapli Kebabs, packed with aromatic spices and bold flavors!

Tavuk Şiş (Turkish Chicken Kebab)

Ingredients:

- 1.5 pounds boneless, skinless chicken breast or thigh, cut into bite-sized cubes
- 1 onion, grated
- 4 cloves garlic, minced
- Juice of 1 lemon
- 1/4 cup olive oil
- 1 teaspoon paprika
- 1 teaspoon ground cumin
- 1 teaspoon ground coriander
- 1 teaspoon dried oregano
- 1 teaspoon dried thyme
- 1 teaspoon salt, or to taste
- 1/2 teaspoon black pepper
- Wooden skewers, soaked in water for at least 30 minutes

Instructions:

1. In a large mixing bowl, combine the grated onion, minced garlic, lemon juice, olive oil, paprika, cumin, coriander, oregano, thyme, salt, and black pepper. Mix well to make the marinade.
2. Add the chicken cubes to the marinade and toss until well coated. Cover the bowl and refrigerate for at least 2 hours, or preferably overnight, to allow the flavors to meld.
3. Preheat your grill to medium-high heat. If using charcoal, wait until the coals are ashed over.
4. Thread the marinated chicken cubes onto the soaked wooden skewers, leaving a little space between each piece.
5. Brush the grill grates lightly with oil to prevent sticking. Place the skewers on the grill and cook for 6-8 minutes, turning occasionally, until the chicken is cooked through and has nice grill marks.
6. Once cooked, remove the skewers from the grill and let them rest for a few minutes before serving.
7. Serve the Tavuk Şiş hot with rice, flatbread, grilled vegetables, and a squeeze of lemon juice if desired.

Enjoy your homemade Tavuk Şiş, a delightful Turkish chicken kebab bursting with flavor!

Shish Kebab (Classic Skewered Meat)

Ingredients:

- 1.5 pounds boneless meat (beef, lamb, or chicken), cut into 1-inch cubes
- 1 onion, finely chopped
- 2 cloves garlic, minced
- Juice of 1 lemon
- 2 tablespoons olive oil
- 1 teaspoon paprika
- 1 teaspoon ground cumin
- 1 teaspoon ground coriander
- 1 teaspoon dried oregano
- 1 teaspoon salt, or to taste
- 1/2 teaspoon black pepper
- Wooden skewers, soaked in water for at least 30 minutes

Instructions:

1. In a large mixing bowl, combine the finely chopped onion, minced garlic, lemon juice, olive oil, paprika, cumin, coriander, oregano, salt, and black pepper. Mix well to make the marinade.
2. Add the meat cubes to the marinade and toss until well coated. Cover the bowl and refrigerate for at least 2 hours, or preferably overnight, to allow the flavors to meld.
3. Preheat your grill to medium-high heat. If using charcoal, wait until the coals are ashed over.
4. Thread the marinated meat cubes onto the soaked wooden skewers, leaving a little space between each piece.
5. Brush the grill grates lightly with oil to prevent sticking. Place the skewers on the grill and cook for 8-10 minutes, turning occasionally, until the meat is cooked through and has nice grill marks.
6. Once cooked, remove the skewers from the grill and let them rest for a few minutes before serving.
7. Serve the Shish Kebab hot with rice, flatbread, grilled vegetables, and a squeeze of lemon juice if desired.

Enjoy your homemade Shish Kebab, a timeless favorite that's perfect for grilling outdoors!

Koobideh Barg (Ground Beef Fillet Kebab)

Ingredients:

- 1 pound ground beef
- 1/2 pound filet mignon, finely chopped or ground
- 1 onion, grated
- 2 cloves garlic, minced
- 1 egg
- 1 tablespoon plain yogurt
- Juice of 1 lemon
- 2 tablespoons olive oil
- 1 teaspoon ground saffron (dissolved in 2 tablespoons hot water)
- 1 teaspoon ground turmeric
- 1 teaspoon ground black pepper
- 1 teaspoon salt, or to taste

Instructions:

1. In a large mixing bowl, combine the ground beef, finely chopped or ground filet mignon, grated onion, minced garlic, egg, yogurt, lemon juice, olive oil, saffron water, turmeric, black pepper, and salt. Mix well until all ingredients are thoroughly combined.
2. Cover the bowl with plastic wrap and refrigerate for at least 1 hour to allow the flavors to meld.
3. Preheat your grill to medium-high heat. If using charcoal, wait until the coals are ashed over.
4. Divide the meat mixture into equal portions and shape each portion into a long, cylindrical sausage shape, about 1 inch in diameter.
5. Brush the grill grates lightly with oil to prevent sticking. Place the shaped meat portions onto the grill and cook for 5-6 minutes per side, or until the kebabs are cooked through and have nice grill marks.
6. Once cooked, remove the kebabs from the grill and let them rest for a few minutes before serving.
7. Serve the Koobideh Barg hot with rice, flatbread, grilled vegetables, and a squeeze of lemon juice if desired.

Enjoy your homemade Koobideh Barg, featuring the perfect blend of ground beef and filet mignon flavors!

Koobideh Saffron (Saffron-infused Ground Meat Kebab)

Ingredients:

- 1 pound ground beef or lamb
- 1 onion, grated
- 2 cloves garlic, minced
- 1 egg
- 1 tablespoon plain yogurt
- Juice of 1 lemon
- 2 tablespoons olive oil
- 1 teaspoon ground saffron (dissolved in 2 tablespoons hot water)
- 1 teaspoon ground turmeric
- 1 teaspoon ground black pepper
- 1 teaspoon salt, or to taste

Instructions:

1. In a large mixing bowl, combine the ground meat, grated onion, minced garlic, egg, yogurt, lemon juice, olive oil, saffron water, turmeric, black pepper, and salt. Mix well until all ingredients are thoroughly combined.
2. Cover the bowl with plastic wrap and refrigerate for at least 1 hour to allow the flavors to meld.
3. Preheat your grill to medium-high heat. If using charcoal, wait until the coals are ashed over.
4. Divide the meat mixture into equal portions and shape each portion into a long, cylindrical sausage shape, about 1 inch in diameter.
5. Brush the grill grates lightly with oil to prevent sticking. Place the shaped meat portions onto the grill and cook for 5-6 minutes per side, or until the kebabs are cooked through and have nice grill marks.
6. Once cooked, remove the kebabs from the grill and let them rest for a few minutes before serving.
7. Serve the Koobideh Saffron hot with rice, flatbread, grilled vegetables, and a squeeze of lemon juice if desired.

Enjoy your homemade Koobideh Saffron, infused with the delicate flavor and vibrant color of saffron!

Persian Rice with Saffron Kebab

Ingredients:

For Persian Rice:

- 2 cups basmati rice
- 4 cups water
- 1 tablespoon salt
- 1/4 teaspoon ground saffron threads (dissolved in 2 tablespoons hot water)
- 2 tablespoons butter or ghee

For Kebabs (Choose your favorite type, such as Koobideh, Joojeh, or Barg):

- 1 pound ground meat (beef, lamb, or chicken)
- 1 onion, grated
- 2 cloves garlic, minced
- 1 teaspoon ground turmeric
- 1 teaspoon ground cumin
- 1 teaspoon ground coriander
- 1 teaspoon salt, or to taste
- 1/2 teaspoon black pepper
- Wooden skewers, soaked in water for at least 30 minutes

Instructions:

1. Rinse the basmati rice under cold water until the water runs clear. This helps remove excess starch.
2. In a large pot, bring 4 cups of water to a boil. Add the salt and rinsed rice. Cook the rice for about 6-7 minutes, stirring occasionally, until it's partially cooked but still firm to the bite. Drain the rice in a fine-mesh sieve and set aside.
3. In the same pot, melt the butter or ghee over low heat. Add half of the saffron water to the bottom of the pot, spreading it evenly.
4. Arrange the soaked wooden skewers in the pot with the saffron water, making sure they are evenly spaced.
5. Place the partially cooked rice on top of the skewers, forming a mound in the center of the pot.
6. Using the handle of a wooden spoon, poke several holes in the rice mound to allow steam to escape.

7. Drizzle the remaining saffron water over the rice mound, covering it evenly.
8. Cover the pot with a lid wrapped in a clean kitchen towel (to absorb excess moisture) and steam the rice over low heat for about 30-40 minutes, or until the rice is fully cooked and fluffy.
9. While the rice is cooking, prepare your favorite type of kebabs using the ground meat and spices. Shape the meat mixture onto skewers and grill them according to your preferred method until cooked through.
10. Once the rice is done, remove the pot from the heat and let it rest for a few minutes.
11. To serve, gently fluff the rice with a fork and transfer it to a serving platter. Arrange the grilled kebabs on top of the rice.
12. Garnish with additional saffron threads and serve hot.

Enjoy your flavorful Persian Rice with Saffron Kebab, a delicious and aromatic dish!

Baghali Polo with Lamb Kebab (Rice with Fava Beans and Lamb Kebab)

Ingredients:

For Baghali Polo (Rice with Fava Beans):

- 2 cups basmati rice
- 1 cup shelled fava beans (fresh or frozen)
- 1/4 cup chopped fresh dill
- 1 onion, finely chopped
- 2 tablespoons butter or ghee
- 1/4 teaspoon ground saffron threads (dissolved in 2 tablespoons hot water)
- Salt to taste

For Lamb Kebab:

- 1 pound lamb meat, cut into cubes
- 1 onion, grated
- 2 cloves garlic, minced
- 1 tablespoon plain yogurt
- Juice of 1 lemon
- 2 tablespoons olive oil
- 1 teaspoon ground cumin
- 1 teaspoon ground coriander
- 1 teaspoon ground black pepper
- 1 teaspoon salt, or to taste
- Wooden skewers, soaked in water for at least 30 minutes

Instructions:

1. Rinse the basmati rice under cold water until the water runs clear. This helps remove excess starch. Soak the rice in water for about 30 minutes, then drain.
2. In a large pot, bring 4 cups of water to a boil. Add the drained rice and cook for about 6-7 minutes, stirring occasionally, until it's partially cooked but still firm to the bite. Drain the rice in a fine-mesh sieve and set aside.
3. In the same pot, melt the butter or ghee over low heat. Add the chopped onion and sauté until translucent.
4. Add the shelled fava beans and chopped dill to the pot with the onions. Cook for 2-3 minutes, stirring occasionally.

5. Spread half of the partially cooked rice over the fava bean mixture in the pot.
6. Drizzle half of the saffron water over the rice layer, then add the remaining rice on top.
7. Drizzle the remaining saffron water over the rice. Cover the pot with a lid wrapped in a clean kitchen towel and steam the rice over low heat for about 30-40 minutes, or until the rice is fully cooked and fluffy.
8. While the rice is cooking, prepare the lamb kebabs. In a mixing bowl, combine the grated onion, minced garlic, yogurt, lemon juice, olive oil, ground cumin, ground coriander, black pepper, and salt. Add the lamb cubes and toss until well coated. Cover and marinate for at least 30 minutes.
9. Preheat your grill to medium-high heat. Thread the marinated lamb cubes onto the soaked wooden skewers.
10. Grill the lamb kebabs for 8-10 minutes, turning occasionally, until they are cooked through and have nice grill marks.
11. Once the rice and kebabs are ready, remove them from heat and let them rest for a few minutes.
12. To serve, gently fluff the rice with a fork and transfer it to a serving platter. Arrange the grilled lamb kebabs on top of the rice.
13. Garnish with additional chopped dill, if desired, and serve hot.

Enjoy your flavorful Baghali Polo with Lamb Kebab, a delicious and aromatic Iranian dish!

Zereshk Polo with Chicken Kebab (Barberry Rice with Chicken Kebab)

Ingredients:

For Zereshk Polo (Barberry Rice):

- 2 cups basmati rice
- 1 cup dried barberries (zereshk)
- 1 onion, finely chopped
- 2 tablespoons butter or ghee
- 1/4 teaspoon ground saffron threads (dissolved in 2 tablespoons hot water)
- 1/4 cup slivered almonds or pistachios (optional, for garnish)
- Salt to taste

For Chicken Kebab:

- 1 pound boneless, skinless chicken breast or thigh, cut into bite-sized pieces
- 1 onion, grated
- 2 cloves garlic, minced
- 1 tablespoon plain yogurt
- Juice of 1 lemon
- 2 tablespoons olive oil
- 1 teaspoon ground turmeric
- 1 teaspoon ground cumin
- 1 teaspoon ground coriander
- 1 teaspoon ground black pepper
- 1 teaspoon salt, or to taste
- Wooden skewers, soaked in water for at least 30 minutes

Instructions:

For Zereshk Polo (Barberry Rice):

1. Rinse the basmati rice under cold water until the water runs clear. This helps remove excess starch. Soak the rice in water for about 30 minutes, then drain.
2. In a large pot, bring 4 cups of water to a boil. Add the drained rice and cook for about 6-7 minutes, stirring occasionally, until it's partially cooked but still firm to the bite. Drain the rice in a fine-mesh sieve and set aside.
3. In a separate pan, heat 1 tablespoon of butter or ghee over medium heat. Add the chopped onion and sauté until translucent.

4. Add the dried barberries to the pan with the onions. Cook for 2-3 minutes, stirring occasionally.
5. Spread half of the partially cooked rice over the barberry mixture in the pan.
6. Drizzle half of the saffron water over the rice layer, then add the remaining rice on top.
7. Drizzle the remaining saffron water over the rice. Cover the pan with a lid wrapped in a clean kitchen towel and steam the rice over low heat for about 30-40 minutes, or until the rice is fully cooked and fluffy.
8. While the rice is cooking, prepare the chicken kebabs. In a mixing bowl, combine the grated onion, minced garlic, yogurt, lemon juice, olive oil, ground turmeric, ground cumin, ground coriander, black pepper, and salt. Add the chicken pieces and toss until well coated. Cover and marinate for at least 30 minutes.
9. Preheat your grill to medium-high heat. Thread the marinated chicken pieces onto the soaked wooden skewers.
10. Grill the chicken kebabs for 8-10 minutes, turning occasionally, until they are cooked through and have nice grill marks.
11. Once the rice and kebabs are ready, remove them from heat and let them rest for a few minutes.
12. To serve, gently fluff the rice with a fork and transfer it to a serving platter. Arrange the grilled chicken kebabs on top of the rice.
13. Garnish with slivered almonds or pistachios, if desired, and serve hot.

Enjoy your flavorful Zereshk Polo with Chicken Kebab, a delicious and aromatic Iranian dish!

Albaloo Polo with Beef Kebab (Sour Cherry Rice with Beef Kebab)

Ingredients:

For Albaloo Polo (Sour Cherry Rice):

- 2 cups basmati rice
- 1 cup dried sour cherries (albaloo)
- 1 onion, finely chopped
- 2 tablespoons butter or ghee
- 1/4 teaspoon ground saffron threads (dissolved in 2 tablespoons hot water)
- 1/4 cup slivered almonds or pistachios (optional, for garnish)
- Salt to taste

For Beef Kebab:

- 1 pound beef (such as sirloin or tenderloin), cut into cubes
- 1 onion, grated
- 2 cloves garlic, minced
- 1 tablespoon plain yogurt
- Juice of 1 lemon
- 2 tablespoons olive oil
- 1 teaspoon ground cumin
- 1 teaspoon ground coriander
- 1 teaspoon ground black pepper
- 1 teaspoon salt, or to taste
- Wooden skewers, soaked in water for at least 30 minutes

Instructions:

For Albaloo Polo (Sour Cherry Rice):

1. Rinse the basmati rice under cold water until the water runs clear. This helps remove excess starch. Soak the rice in water for about 30 minutes, then drain.
2. In a large pot, bring 4 cups of water to a boil. Add the drained rice and cook for about 6-7 minutes, stirring occasionally, until it's partially cooked but still firm to the bite. Drain the rice in a fine-mesh sieve and set aside.
3. In a separate pan, heat 1 tablespoon of butter or ghee over medium heat. Add the chopped onion and sauté until translucent.

4. Add the dried sour cherries to the pan with the onions. Cook for 2-3 minutes, stirring occasionally.
5. Spread half of the partially cooked rice over the sour cherry mixture in the pan.
6. Drizzle half of the saffron water over the rice layer, then add the remaining rice on top.
7. Drizzle the remaining saffron water over the rice. Cover the pan with a lid wrapped in a clean kitchen towel and steam the rice over low heat for about 30-40 minutes, or until the rice is fully cooked and fluffy.
8. While the rice is cooking, prepare the beef kebabs. In a mixing bowl, combine the grated onion, minced garlic, yogurt, lemon juice, olive oil, ground cumin, ground coriander, black pepper, and salt. Add the beef cubes and toss until well coated. Cover and marinate for at least 30 minutes.
9. Preheat your grill to medium-high heat. Thread the marinated beef cubes onto the soaked wooden skewers.
10. Grill the beef kebabs for 8-10 minutes, turning occasionally, until they are cooked through and have nice grill marks.
11. Once the rice and kebabs are ready, remove them from heat and let them rest for a few minutes.
12. To serve, gently fluff the rice with a fork and transfer it to a serving platter. Arrange the grilled beef kebabs on top of the rice.
13. Garnish with slivered almonds or pistachios, if desired, and serve hot.

Enjoy your flavorful Albaloo Polo with Beef Kebab, a delicious and aromatic Iranian dish!

Lubia Polo with Joojeh Kebab (Green Bean Rice with Grilled Chicken)

Ingredients:

For Lubia Polo (Green Bean Rice):

- 2 cups basmati rice
- 1 cup green beans, trimmed and cut into bite-sized pieces
- 1 onion, finely chopped
- 2 tablespoons butter or ghee
- 1/4 teaspoon ground saffron threads (dissolved in 2 tablespoons hot water)
- 1/4 cup slivered almonds or pistachios (optional, for garnish)
- Salt to taste

For Joojeh Kebab (Grilled Chicken):

- 4 boneless, skinless chicken breasts
- 1 onion, grated
- 2 cloves garlic, minced
- 1/4 cup plain yogurt
- Juice of 1 lemon
- 2 tablespoons olive oil
- 1 teaspoon ground saffron (dissolved in 2 tablespoons hot water)
- 1 teaspoon ground turmeric
- 1 teaspoon ground cumin
- 1 teaspoon ground coriander
- 1 teaspoon salt, or to taste

Instructions:

For Lubia Polo (Green Bean Rice):

1. Rinse the basmati rice under cold water until the water runs clear. This helps remove excess starch. Soak the rice in water for about 30 minutes, then drain.
2. In a large pot, bring 4 cups of water to a boil. Add the drained rice and cook for about 6-7 minutes, stirring occasionally, until it's partially cooked but still firm to the bite. Drain the rice in a fine-mesh sieve and set aside.
3. In a separate pan, heat 1 tablespoon of butter or ghee over medium heat. Add the chopped onion and sauté until translucent.

4. Add the green beans to the pan with the onions. Cook for 2-3 minutes, stirring occasionally.
5. Spread half of the partially cooked rice over the green bean mixture in the pan.
6. Drizzle half of the saffron water over the rice layer, then add the remaining rice on top.
7. Drizzle the remaining saffron water over the rice. Cover the pan with a lid wrapped in a clean kitchen towel and steam the rice over low heat for about 30-40 minutes, or until the rice is fully cooked and fluffy.
8. While the rice is cooking, prepare the Joojeh Kebab. In a mixing bowl, combine the grated onion, minced garlic, yogurt, lemon juice, olive oil, ground saffron, turmeric, cumin, coriander, and salt. Add the chicken breasts and toss until well coated. Cover and marinate for at least 30 minutes.
9. Preheat your grill to medium-high heat. Grill the marinated chicken breasts for 6-8 minutes per side, or until they are cooked through and have nice grill marks.
10. Once the rice and chicken are ready, remove them from heat and let them rest for a few minutes.
11. To serve, gently fluff the rice with a fork and transfer it to a serving platter. Arrange the grilled chicken breasts on top of the rice.
12. Garnish with slivered almonds or pistachios, if desired, and serve hot.

Enjoy your flavorful Lubia Polo with Joojeh Kebab, a delicious and aromatic Iranian dish!

Shirin Polo with Kubideh Kebab (Sweet Rice with Ground Meat Kebab)

Ingredients:

For Shirin Polo (Sweet Rice):

- 2 cups basmati rice
- 1/2 cup mixed dried fruits (such as raisins, chopped apricots, and chopped dates)
- 1/4 cup slivered almonds or pistachios
- 1 onion, finely chopped
- 2 tablespoons butter or ghee
- 1/4 teaspoon ground saffron threads (dissolved in 2 tablespoons hot water)
- 1/4 teaspoon ground cinnamon
- 1/4 teaspoon ground cardamom
- 1/4 cup honey or granulated sugar
- Salt to taste

For Kubideh Kebab (Ground Meat Kebab):

- 1 pound ground beef or lamb
- 1 onion, grated
- 2 cloves garlic, minced
- 1 tablespoon plain yogurt
- Juice of 1 lemon
- 2 tablespoons olive oil
- 1 teaspoon ground turmeric
- 1 teaspoon ground cumin
- 1 teaspoon ground coriander
- 1 teaspoon ground black pepper
- 1 teaspoon salt, or to taste
- Wooden skewers, soaked in water for at least 30 minutes

Instructions:

For Shirin Polo (Sweet Rice):

1. Rinse the basmati rice under cold water until the water runs clear. This helps remove excess starch. Soak the rice in water for about 30 minutes, then drain.

2. In a large pot, bring 4 cups of water to a boil. Add the drained rice and cook for about 6-7 minutes, stirring occasionally, until it's partially cooked but still firm to the bite. Drain the rice in a fine-mesh sieve and set aside.
3. In a separate pan, heat 1 tablespoon of butter or ghee over medium heat. Add the chopped onion and sauté until translucent.
4. Add the mixed dried fruits and slivered almonds or pistachios to the pan with the onions. Cook for 2-3 minutes, stirring occasionally.
5. Spread half of the partially cooked rice over the fruit and nut mixture in the pan.
6. Sprinkle half of the saffron water, ground cinnamon, and ground cardamom over the rice layer, then add the remaining rice on top.
7. Sprinkle the remaining saffron water, ground cinnamon, and ground cardamom over the rice. Drizzle honey or sprinkle sugar evenly over the rice.
8. Cover the pan with a lid wrapped in a clean kitchen towel and steam the rice over low heat for about 30-40 minutes, or until the rice is fully cooked and fluffy.

For Kubideh Kebab (Ground Meat Kebab):

1. In a mixing bowl, combine the grated onion, minced garlic, yogurt, lemon juice, olive oil, ground turmeric, cumin, coriander, black pepper, and salt. Add the ground beef or lamb and mix until well combined.
2. Divide the meat mixture into equal portions and shape each portion into a long, cylindrical sausage shape, about 1 inch in diameter. Thread the meat onto the soaked wooden skewers.
3. Preheat your grill to medium-high heat. Grill the kebabs for 5-6 minutes per side, or until they are cooked through and have nice grill marks.
4. Once the rice and kebabs are ready, remove them from heat and let them rest for a few minutes.

To serve:

1. Gently fluff the sweet rice with a fork and transfer it to a serving platter.
2. Arrange the grilled Kubideh Kebabs on top of the rice.
3. Garnish with additional slivered almonds or pistachios, if desired.

Enjoy your flavorful Shirin Polo with Kubideh Kebab, a delicious and aromatic Iranian dish!

Adas Polo with Barg Kebab (Lentil Rice with Filet Mignon Kebab)

Ingredients:

For Adas Polo (Lentil Rice):

- 2 cups basmati rice
- 1 cup lentils (green or brown), rinsed
- 1 onion, finely chopped
- 2 tablespoons butter or ghee
- 1/4 teaspoon ground saffron threads (dissolved in 2 tablespoons hot water)
- 1/4 cup slivered almonds or pistachios
- Salt to taste

For Barg Kebab (Filet Mignon Kebab):

- 1 pound filet mignon, cut into cubes
- 1 onion, grated
- 2 cloves garlic, minced
- 1 tablespoon plain yogurt
- Juice of 1 lemon
- 2 tablespoons olive oil
- 1 teaspoon ground saffron (dissolved in 2 tablespoons hot water)
- 1 teaspoon ground turmeric
- 1 teaspoon ground cumin
- 1 teaspoon ground coriander
- 1 teaspoon ground black pepper
- 1 teaspoon salt, or to taste
- Wooden skewers, soaked in water for at least 30 minutes

Instructions:

For Adas Polo (Lentil Rice):

1. Rinse the basmati rice under cold water until the water runs clear. This helps remove excess starch. Soak the rice in water for about 30 minutes, then drain.

2. In a large pot, bring 4 cups of water to a boil. Add the drained rice and lentils, and cook for about 6-7 minutes, stirring occasionally, until they're partially cooked but still firm to the bite. Drain the rice and lentils in a fine-mesh sieve and set aside.
3. In a separate pan, heat 1 tablespoon of butter or ghee over medium heat. Add the chopped onion and sauté until translucent.
4. Spread half of the partially cooked rice and lentil mixture over the onions in the pan.
5. Sprinkle half of the saffron water and slivered almonds or pistachios over the rice and lentil layer, then add the remaining rice and lentils on top.
6. Sprinkle the remaining saffron water and slivered almonds or pistachios over the rice and lentils. Drizzle with the remaining butter or ghee.
7. Cover the pan with a lid wrapped in a clean kitchen towel and steam the rice and lentils over low heat for about 30-40 minutes, or until they're fully cooked and fluffy.

For Barg Kebab (Filet Mignon Kebab):

1. In a mixing bowl, combine the grated onion, minced garlic, yogurt, lemon juice, olive oil, ground saffron, turmeric, cumin, coriander, black pepper, and salt. Add the filet mignon cubes and mix until well coated. Cover and marinate for at least 30 minutes.
2. Preheat your grill to medium-high heat. Thread the marinated filet mignon cubes onto the soaked wooden skewers.
3. Grill the kebabs for 4-5 minutes per side, or until they're cooked through and have nice grill marks.
4. Once the rice and kebabs are ready, remove them from heat and let them rest for a few minutes.

To serve:

1. Gently fluff the lentil rice with a fork and transfer it to a serving platter.
2. Arrange the grilled Barg Kebabs on top of the rice.
3. Garnish with additional slivered almonds or pistachios, if desired.

Enjoy your delicious Adas Polo with Barg Kebab, a flavorful Iranian dish!

Kebab-e Masti (Creamy Kebab)

Ingredients:

For Kebab-e Masti (Creamy Kebab):

- 1 pound ground beef or lamb
- 1 onion, grated
- 2 cloves garlic, minced
- 1/4 cup plain yogurt
- Juice of 1 lemon
- 2 tablespoons olive oil
- 1 teaspoon ground turmeric
- 1 teaspoon ground cumin
- 1 teaspoon ground coriander
- 1 teaspoon ground black pepper
- 1 teaspoon salt, or to taste
- 1/2 cup heavy cream
- 1/4 cup chopped fresh parsley or cilantro (for garnish)

Instructions:

1. In a mixing bowl, combine the grated onion, minced garlic, yogurt, lemon juice, olive oil, ground turmeric, cumin, coriander, black pepper, and salt. Add the ground beef or lamb and mix until well combined. Cover and refrigerate the mixture for at least 30 minutes to allow the flavors to meld.
2. Preheat your grill to medium-high heat. Shape the marinated meat mixture into long, cylindrical sausage shapes or onto skewers.
3. Grill the kebabs for 8-10 minutes, turning occasionally, until they are cooked through and have nice grill marks.
4. Once the kebabs are cooked, transfer them to a serving platter and keep warm.
5. In a small saucepan, heat the heavy cream over low heat until it's warm but not boiling.
6. Pour the warm cream over the grilled kebabs, covering them evenly.
7. Garnish the kebabs with chopped fresh parsley or cilantro.
8. Serve the Kebab-e Masti hot with rice, bread, or salad.

Enjoy your creamy and flavorful Kebab-e Masti, a delicious Iranian delicacy!

Kebab Kubideh (Ground Beef Kebab)

Ingredients:

- 1 pound ground beef (preferably lean)
- 1 onion, grated
- 2 cloves garlic, minced
- 1 tablespoon plain yogurt
- Juice of 1 lemon
- 2 tablespoons olive oil
- 1 teaspoon ground turmeric
- 1 teaspoon ground cumin
- 1 teaspoon ground coriander
- 1 teaspoon ground black pepper
- 1 teaspoon salt, or to taste
- Wooden skewers, soaked in water for at least 30 minutes

Instructions:

1. In a mixing bowl, combine the grated onion, minced garlic, yogurt, lemon juice, olive oil, ground turmeric, cumin, coriander, black pepper, and salt. Mix well to form a marinade.
2. Add the ground beef to the marinade mixture and mix until all ingredients are evenly incorporated.
3. Cover the bowl with plastic wrap and refrigerate for at least 30 minutes to allow the flavors to meld.
4. Preheat your grill to medium-high heat. If using charcoal, wait until the coals are ashed over.
5. Take a handful of the marinated ground beef mixture and shape it onto a skewer, forming a long, cylindrical sausage shape. Repeat with the remaining mixture and skewers.
6. Lightly oil the grill grates to prevent sticking. Place the skewers of ground beef onto the grill and cook for 5-6 minutes per side, or until the kebabs are cooked through and have nice grill marks.
7. Once cooked, remove the kebabs from the grill and let them rest for a few minutes before serving.
8. Serve the Kebab Kubideh hot with rice, bread, grilled vegetables, or salad.

Enjoy your delicious and flavorful Kebab Kubideh, a classic Iranian dish!

Jigar Kebab (Liver Kebab)

Ingredients:

- 1 pound beef liver, sliced into thin strips
- 1 onion, grated
- 2 cloves garlic, minced
- Juice of 1 lemon
- 2 tablespoons olive oil
- 1 teaspoon ground turmeric
- 1 teaspoon ground cumin
- 1 teaspoon ground coriander
- 1 teaspoon ground black pepper
- 1 teaspoon salt, or to taste
- Wooden skewers, soaked in water for at least 30 minutes

Instructions:

1. In a mixing bowl, combine the grated onion, minced garlic, lemon juice, olive oil, ground turmeric, cumin, coriander, black pepper, and salt. Mix well to form a marinade.
2. Add the sliced beef liver to the marinade mixture and coat each piece evenly. Cover the bowl with plastic wrap and refrigerate for at least 1 hour to allow the flavors to meld.
3. Preheat your grill to medium-high heat. If using charcoal, wait until the coals are ashed over.
4. Thread the marinated liver slices onto the soaked wooden skewers, ensuring they are evenly distributed.
5. Lightly oil the grill grates to prevent sticking. Place the skewers of liver onto the grill and cook for 3-4 minutes per side, or until the liver is cooked through and has nice grill marks.
6. Once cooked, remove the liver kebabs from the grill and let them rest for a few minutes before serving.
7. Serve the Jigar Kebab hot with rice, bread, grilled vegetables, or salad.

Enjoy your delicious and tender Jigar Kebab, a delightful dish that's rich in flavor!

Kebab Tabei (Pan-Fried Kebab)

Ingredients:

- 1 pound ground beef or lamb
- 1 onion, grated
- 2 cloves garlic, minced
- 1 tablespoon plain yogurt
- Juice of 1 lemon
- 2 tablespoons olive oil
- 1 teaspoon ground turmeric
- 1 teaspoon ground cumin
- 1 teaspoon ground coriander
- 1 teaspoon ground black pepper
- 1 teaspoon salt, or to taste
- 2 tablespoons chopped fresh parsley or cilantro (optional, for garnish)
- Cooking oil (for frying)

Instructions:

1. In a mixing bowl, combine the grated onion, minced garlic, yogurt, lemon juice, olive oil, ground turmeric, cumin, coriander, black pepper, and salt. Mix well to form a marinade.
2. Add the ground beef or lamb to the marinade mixture and mix until all ingredients are evenly incorporated.
3. Cover the bowl with plastic wrap and refrigerate for at least 30 minutes to allow the flavors to meld.
4. After marinating, shape the meat mixture into small oval-shaped kebabs or patties.
5. Heat a few tablespoons of cooking oil in a large frying pan over medium heat.
6. Once the oil is hot, add the kebabs to the pan in a single layer, making sure not to overcrowd the pan. You may need to cook the kebabs in batches depending on the size of your pan.
7. Cook the kebabs for 4-5 minutes on each side, or until they are browned and cooked through.
8. Once cooked, transfer the kebabs to a plate lined with paper towels to drain any excess oil.
9. Garnish the Kebab Tabei with chopped fresh parsley or cilantro, if desired.

10. Serve the Kebab Tabei hot with rice, bread, yogurt, or salad.

Enjoy your delicious and flavorful Pan-Fried Kebab Tabei!

Kebab-e Torki (Turkish Kebab)

Ingredients:

- 1 pound ground lamb or beef (or a combination of both)
- 1 onion, grated
- 2 cloves garlic, minced
- 1 tablespoon tomato paste
- 1 tablespoon olive oil
- 1 teaspoon ground sumac (optional)
- 1 teaspoon ground cumin
- 1 teaspoon paprika
- 1 teaspoon Aleppo pepper or crushed red pepper flakes (adjust to taste)
- 1 teaspoon salt, or to taste
- Wooden skewers, soaked in water for at least 30 minutes

Instructions:

1. In a large mixing bowl, combine the grated onion, minced garlic, tomato paste, olive oil, ground sumac (if using), ground cumin, paprika, Aleppo pepper or crushed red pepper flakes, and salt. Mix well to form a marinade.
2. Add the ground lamb or beef to the marinade mixture and mix until thoroughly combined. Cover the bowl with plastic wrap and refrigerate for at least 1 hour to allow the flavors to meld.
3. Preheat your grill to medium-high heat. If using charcoal, wait until the coals are ashed over.
4. Take a handful of the marinated meat mixture and shape it onto a skewer, forming a long, sausage-like shape. Repeat with the remaining mixture and skewers.
5. Lightly oil the grill grates to prevent sticking. Place the skewers of meat onto the grill and cook for 5-6 minutes per side, or until the kebabs are cooked through and have nice grill marks.
6. Once cooked, remove the kebabs from the grill and let them rest for a few minutes before serving.
7. Serve the Turkish Adana Kebabs hot with rice, bread, grilled vegetables, or salad.

Enjoy your delicious and flavorful Turkish Kebab!

Kebab-e Morgh (Chicken Kebab)

Ingredients:

- 1.5 pounds boneless, skinless chicken breasts or thighs, cut into bite-sized pieces
- 1 onion, grated
- 3 cloves garlic, minced
- Juice of 1 lemon
- 2 tablespoons plain yogurt
- 2 tablespoons olive oil
- 1 teaspoon ground turmeric
- 1 teaspoon ground cumin
- 1 teaspoon ground paprika
- 1 teaspoon ground black pepper
- 1 teaspoon salt, or to taste
- Wooden skewers, soaked in water for at least 30 minutes

Instructions:

1. In a mixing bowl, combine the grated onion, minced garlic, lemon juice, yogurt, olive oil, ground turmeric, cumin, paprika, black pepper, and salt. Mix well to form a marinade.
2. Add the chicken pieces to the marinade mixture and toss until they are evenly coated. Cover the bowl with plastic wrap and refrigerate for at least 1 hour, or overnight for best results, to allow the flavors to meld.
3. Preheat your grill to medium-high heat. If using charcoal, wait until the coals are ashed over.
4. Thread the marinated chicken pieces onto the soaked wooden skewers, making sure they are evenly distributed.
5. Lightly oil the grill grates to prevent sticking. Place the skewers of chicken onto the grill and cook for 6-8 minutes per side, or until the chicken is cooked through and has nice grill marks.
6. Once cooked, remove the chicken kebabs from the grill and let them rest for a few minutes before serving.
7. Serve the Kebab-e Morgh hot with rice, bread, grilled vegetables, or salad.

Enjoy your delicious and flavorful Chicken Kebab!

Gheymeh Kebab (Split Pea Stew with Kebab)

Ingredients:

For the Split Pea Stew (Gheymeh):

- 1 cup yellow split peas, rinsed and drained
- 1 onion, finely chopped
- 2 cloves garlic, minced
- 2 tablespoons tomato paste
- 2 tablespoons vegetable oil
- 1 teaspoon ground turmeric
- 1 teaspoon ground cinnamon
- 1/2 teaspoon ground cumin
- Salt and pepper to taste
- 4 cups water or vegetable broth
- 1 tablespoon dried lime powder (limoo amani) or the juice of 1 fresh lime
- 1 tablespoon dried fenugreek leaves (optional)
- 1 large potato, peeled and cut into cubes
- 1 tablespoon dried barberry (zereshk) for garnish (optional)

For the Kebab:

- 1 pound ground beef or lamb
- 1 onion, grated
- 2 cloves garlic, minced
- 1 tablespoon plain yogurt
- Juice of 1 lemon
- 2 tablespoons olive oil
- 1 teaspoon ground turmeric
- 1 teaspoon ground cumin
- 1 teaspoon ground coriander
- 1 teaspoon ground black pepper
- 1 teaspoon salt, or to taste
- Wooden skewers, soaked in water for at least 30 minutes

Instructions:

1. To make the split pea stew (Gheymeh), heat vegetable oil in a large pot over medium heat. Add the chopped onion and minced garlic, and sauté until golden brown.
2. Add the tomato paste, ground turmeric, ground cinnamon, ground cumin, salt, and pepper to the pot. Cook for another 2-3 minutes, stirring frequently.
3. Add the rinsed split peas and cubed potato to the pot, along with water or vegetable broth. Bring to a boil, then reduce the heat to low and let simmer, partially covered, for about 45 minutes to 1 hour, or until the split peas are tender and the stew has thickened.
4. Meanwhile, prepare the kebab. In a mixing bowl, combine the grated onion, minced garlic, yogurt, lemon juice, olive oil, ground turmeric, cumin, coriander, black pepper, and salt. Add the ground beef or lamb and mix until well combined. Cover and refrigerate for at least 30 minutes to allow the flavors to meld.
5. Preheat your grill to medium-high heat. Shape the marinated meat mixture onto the soaked wooden skewers, forming long, sausage-like shapes.
6. Grill the kebabs for 5-6 minutes per side, or until cooked through and browned on the outside.
7. Once the split pea stew (Gheymeh) is cooked, stir in the dried lime powder or lime juice and dried fenugreek leaves (if using). Adjust the seasoning if necessary.
8. To serve, ladle the split pea stew (Gheymeh) into bowls and top with the grilled kebabs. Garnish with dried barberries (if using) for added flavor and color.

Enjoy your delicious Gheymeh Kebab, a comforting and flavorful Iranian dish!

Bademjan Kebab (Eggplant and Meat Kebab)

Ingredients:

For the Meat Marinade:

- 1 pound beef or lamb, cut into cubes
- 1 onion, grated
- 2 cloves garlic, minced
- Juice of 1 lemon
- 2 tablespoons plain yogurt
- 2 tablespoons olive oil
- 1 teaspoon ground turmeric
- 1 teaspoon ground cumin
- 1 teaspoon ground coriander
- 1 teaspoon ground black pepper
- 1 teaspoon salt, or to taste

For the Eggplant:

- 2 large eggplants
- Salt
- Olive oil for brushing

For the Sauce:

- 1 onion, finely chopped
- 2 tomatoes, chopped
- 2 cloves garlic, minced
- 1 tablespoon tomato paste
- 1 teaspoon ground turmeric
- 1 teaspoon ground cumin
- 1 teaspoon ground coriander
- 1/2 teaspoon ground cinnamon
- Salt and pepper to taste
- 1 cup water or beef broth

Instructions:

1. Start by marinating the meat. In a mixing bowl, combine the grated onion, minced garlic, lemon juice, yogurt, olive oil, ground turmeric, cumin, coriander, black pepper, and salt. Add the cubed meat and toss until well coated. Cover and refrigerate for at least 1 hour, or overnight for best results.
2. Preheat your grill to medium-high heat.
3. Slice the eggplants lengthwise into 1/2-inch thick slices. Place the slices on a baking sheet and sprinkle them with salt. Let them sit for about 15-20 minutes to allow the excess moisture to drain.
4. Pat the eggplant slices dry with paper towels and brush both sides lightly with olive oil.
5. Grill the eggplant slices for about 3-4 minutes per side, or until they are tender and have nice grill marks. Remove from the grill and set aside.
6. Thread the marinated meat cubes onto skewers.
7. Grill the meat skewers for about 4-5 minutes per side, or until they are cooked to your desired level of doneness.
8. While the meat is grilling, prepare the sauce. Heat a bit of olive oil in a skillet over medium heat. Add the chopped onion and cook until softened and translucent.
9. Add the minced garlic, chopped tomatoes, tomato paste, ground turmeric, cumin, coriander, cinnamon, salt, and pepper to the skillet. Cook for a few minutes until the tomatoes break down and release their juices.
10. Pour in the water or beef broth and stir to combine. Bring the sauce to a simmer and let it cook for about 10-15 minutes, or until it thickens slightly.
11. To serve, arrange the grilled eggplant slices on a serving platter and place the grilled meat skewers on top. Pour the sauce over the kebabs and eggplant.
12. Garnish with chopped fresh herbs, such as parsley or cilantro, if desired.

Enjoy your delicious Bademjan Kebab, a flavorful Persian dish!

Baghali Polo with Joojeh Kebab (Rice with Dill and Grilled Chicken)

Ingredients:

For Baghali Polo (Dill Rice with Lima Beans):

- 2 cups basmati rice
- 1 cup fresh dill, chopped
- 1 cup cooked or canned lima beans (baghali), drained
- 1 onion, finely chopped
- 2 tablespoons butter or ghee
- 1/4 teaspoon ground saffron threads (dissolved in 2 tablespoons hot water)
- Salt to taste

For Joojeh Kebab (Grilled Chicken):

- 4 boneless, skinless chicken breasts
- 1 onion, grated
- 2 cloves garlic, minced
- 1/4 cup plain yogurt
- Juice of 1 lemon
- 2 tablespoons olive oil
- 1 teaspoon ground saffron (dissolved in 2 tablespoons hot water)
- 1 teaspoon ground turmeric
- 1 teaspoon ground cumin
- 1 teaspoon ground coriander
- 1 teaspoon salt, or to taste

Instructions:

For Baghali Polo (Dill Rice with Lima Beans):

1. Rinse the basmati rice under cold water until the water runs clear. This helps remove excess starch. Soak the rice in water for about 30 minutes, then drain.
2. In a large pot, bring 4 cups of water to a boil. Add the drained rice and cook for about 6-7 minutes, stirring occasionally, until it's partially cooked but still firm to the bite. Drain the rice in a fine-mesh sieve and set aside.

3. In a separate pan, heat 1 tablespoon of butter or ghee over medium heat. Add the chopped onion and sauté until translucent.
4. Add the chopped dill and lima beans to the pan with the onions. Cook for 2-3 minutes, stirring occasionally.
5. Spread half of the partially cooked rice over the dill and lima bean mixture in the pan.
6. Drizzle half of the saffron water over the rice layer, then add the remaining rice on top.
7. Drizzle the remaining saffron water over the rice. Add the remaining butter or ghee on top of the rice.
8. Cover the pan with a lid wrapped in a clean kitchen towel and steam the rice over low heat for about 30-40 minutes, or until the rice is fully cooked and fluffy.

For Joojeh Kebab (Grilled Chicken):

1. In a mixing bowl, combine the grated onion, minced garlic, yogurt, lemon juice, olive oil, ground saffron, turmeric, cumin, coriander, and salt. Add the chicken breasts and toss until well coated. Cover and marinate for at least 30 minutes.
2. Preheat your grill to medium-high heat. Grill the marinated chicken breasts for 6-8 minutes per side, or until they are cooked through and have nice grill marks.
3. Once the rice and chicken are ready, remove them from heat and let them rest for a few minutes.

To serve:

1. Gently fluff the dill rice with a fork and transfer it to a serving platter.
2. Arrange the grilled chicken breasts on top of the rice.
3. Serve hot and enjoy your delicious Baghali Polo with Joojeh Kebab!

Enjoy this flavorful and aromatic Iranian dish!

Kebab-e Torsh (Sour Kebab)

Ingredients:

For the Marinade:

- 1/4 cup pomegranate molasses
- 1/4 cup olive oil
- 2 tablespoons red wine vinegar
- 2 cloves garlic, minced
- 1 teaspoon ground turmeric
- 1 teaspoon ground sumac
- 1 teaspoon ground cumin
- 1 teaspoon ground coriander
- 1 teaspoon salt, or to taste
- 1/2 teaspoon ground black pepper

For the Kebab:

- 1.5 pounds boneless beef or lamb, cut into cubes
- Wooden skewers, soaked in water for at least 30 minutes

Instructions:

1. In a mixing bowl, combine all the marinade ingredients: pomegranate molasses, olive oil, red wine vinegar, minced garlic, ground turmeric, ground sumac, ground cumin, ground coriander, salt, and ground black pepper. Mix well to combine.
2. Add the cubed meat to the marinade and toss until evenly coated. Cover the bowl with plastic wrap and refrigerate for at least 2 hours, or overnight for best results, to allow the flavors to meld.
3. Preheat your grill to medium-high heat. If using charcoal, wait until the coals are ashed over.
4. Thread the marinated meat onto the soaked wooden skewers, making sure they are evenly distributed.
5. Lightly oil the grill grates to prevent sticking. Place the skewers of meat onto the grill and cook for about 8-10 minutes, turning occasionally, or until the meat is cooked through and has nice grill marks.
6. Once cooked, remove the kebabs from the grill and let them rest for a few minutes before serving.

7. Serve the Kebab-e Torsh hot with rice, bread, grilled vegetables, or salad.

Enjoy the tangy and flavorful taste of Kebab-e Torsh, a delicious Iranian dish!

Zaban Kebab (Tongue Kebab)

Ingredients:

- 2 beef or lamb tongues
- 1 onion, chopped
- 4 cloves garlic, minced
- Juice of 1 lemon
- 2 tablespoons olive oil
- 1 teaspoon ground turmeric
- 1 teaspoon ground cumin
- 1 teaspoon ground coriander
- 1 teaspoon paprika
- 1 teaspoon salt, or to taste
- 1/2 teaspoon ground black pepper

Instructions:

1. Start by preparing the tongues. Rinse them under cold water and place them in a large pot. Cover the tongues with water and bring to a boil over high heat.
2. Once boiling, reduce the heat to low, cover, and let simmer for about 2-3 hours, or until the tongues are tender. You can check for tenderness by piercing the tongues with a fork; they should be easily pierced.
3. Once the tongues are tender, remove them from the pot and let them cool slightly.
4. While the tongues are cooling, prepare the marinade. In a mixing bowl, combine the chopped onion, minced garlic, lemon juice, olive oil, ground turmeric, cumin, coriander, paprika, salt, and black pepper. Mix well to combine.
5. Peel the outer layer of skin from the tongues and discard. Slice the tongues into thick pieces.
6. Place the sliced tongues in the marinade mixture and toss until they are evenly coated. Cover the bowl with plastic wrap and refrigerate for at least 1 hour, or overnight for best results, to allow the flavors to meld.
7. Preheat your grill to medium-high heat. If using charcoal, wait until the coals are ashed over.
8. Thread the marinated tongue pieces onto skewers, making sure they are evenly distributed.

9. Lightly oil the grill grates to prevent sticking. Place the skewers of tongue onto the grill and cook for about 4-5 minutes per side, or until they are heated through and have nice grill marks.
10. Once cooked, remove the tongue kebabs from the grill and let them rest for a few minutes before serving.
11. Serve the Zaban Kebab hot with rice, bread, grilled vegetables, or salad.

Enjoy the tender and flavorful taste of Zaban Kebab, a unique and delicious dish!

Kebab-e Nokhodchi (Chickpea Kebab)

Ingredients:

- 2 cups cooked chickpeas (canned or cooked from dried)
- 1 onion, finely chopped
- 2 cloves garlic, minced
- 1/4 cup fresh parsley, chopped
- 1/4 cup fresh cilantro, chopped
- 1 teaspoon ground cumin
- 1 teaspoon ground coriander
- 1/2 teaspoon ground turmeric
- 1/2 teaspoon paprika
- 1/4 teaspoon cayenne pepper (optional, for heat)
- Salt and pepper to taste
- 2 tablespoons all-purpose flour or chickpea flour (besan)
- Olive oil for frying

Instructions:

1. In a large mixing bowl, mash the cooked chickpeas with a fork or potato masher until they are partially mashed but still have some texture.
2. Add the finely chopped onion, minced garlic, chopped parsley, chopped cilantro, ground cumin, ground coriander, ground turmeric, paprika, cayenne pepper (if using), salt, and pepper to the bowl with the mashed chickpeas. Mix well to combine all the ingredients.
3. Gradually add the flour to the mixture, stirring until it forms a dough-like consistency that holds together when pressed.
4. Shape the chickpea mixture into small, flat patties or cylindrical shapes, similar to traditional kebabs.
5. Heat a few tablespoons of olive oil in a large skillet over medium heat. Once the oil is hot, carefully place the chickpea kebabs in the skillet, making sure not to overcrowd the pan.
6. Cook the kebabs for about 3-4 minutes on each side, or until they are golden brown and crispy on the outside.
7. Once cooked, remove the chickpea kebabs from the skillet and place them on a plate lined with paper towels to absorb any excess oil.

8. Serve the Kebab-e Nokhodchi hot with your favorite sauce, such as tahini sauce or yogurt sauce, and alongside pita bread or rice. You can also enjoy them in wraps or sandwiches.

Enjoy the delicious and nutritious Kebab-e Nokhodchi, a flavorful vegetarian alternative to traditional meat kebabs!

Kebab-e Lari (Lari Kebab)

Ingredients:

- 1 pound ground beef or lamb
- 1 onion, grated
- 2 cloves garlic, minced
- 1 tablespoon plain yogurt
- Juice of 1 lemon
- 2 tablespoons olive oil
- 1 teaspoon ground turmeric
- 1 teaspoon ground cumin
- 1 teaspoon ground coriander
- 1 teaspoon ground black pepper
- 1 teaspoon salt, or to taste
- Wooden skewers, soaked in water for at least 30 minutes

Instructions:

1. In a mixing bowl, combine the grated onion, minced garlic, yogurt, lemon juice, olive oil, ground turmeric, cumin, coriander, black pepper, and salt. Mix well to form a marinade.
2. Add the ground beef or lamb to the marinade mixture and mix until all ingredients are evenly incorporated.
3. Cover the bowl with plastic wrap and refrigerate for at least 30 minutes to allow the flavors to meld.
4. Preheat your grill to medium-high heat. If using charcoal, wait until the coals are ashed over.
5. Take a handful of the marinated meat mixture and shape it onto a skewer, forming a long, sausage-like shape. Repeat with the remaining mixture and skewers.
6. Lightly oil the grill grates to prevent sticking. Place the skewers of meat onto the grill and cook for 5-6 minutes per side, or until the kebabs are cooked through and have nice grill marks.
7. Once cooked, remove the kebabs from the grill and let them rest for a few minutes before serving.
8. Serve the Kebab-e Lari hot with rice, bread, grilled vegetables, or salad.

Enjoy your delicious and flavorful Lari Kebab, a classic Iranian dish!

Kebab-e Borani (Borani Kebab)

Ingredients:

For the Kebabs:

- 1 pound ground beef or lamb
- 1 onion, grated
- 2 cloves garlic, minced
- 1 tablespoon plain yogurt
- Juice of 1 lemon
- 2 tablespoons olive oil
- 1 teaspoon ground turmeric
- 1 teaspoon ground cumin
- 1 teaspoon ground coriander
- 1 teaspoon ground black pepper
- 1 teaspoon salt, or to taste
- Wooden skewers, soaked in water for at least 30 minutes

For the Yogurt Sauce:

- 1 cup plain Greek yogurt
- 2 cloves garlic, minced
- 1 tablespoon dried mint
- Salt and pepper to taste

For the Spinach:

- 1 tablespoon olive oil
- 1 onion, finely chopped
- 4 cups fresh spinach, chopped
- Salt and pepper to taste

Instructions:

1. In a mixing bowl, combine the grated onion, minced garlic, yogurt, lemon juice, olive oil, ground turmeric, cumin, coriander, black pepper, and salt. Mix well to form a marinade.
2. Add the ground beef or lamb to the marinade mixture and mix until all ingredients are evenly incorporated.
3. Cover the bowl with plastic wrap and refrigerate for at least 30 minutes to allow the flavors to meld.
4. Preheat your grill to medium-high heat. If using charcoal, wait until the coals are ashed over.
5. Take a handful of the marinated meat mixture and shape it onto a skewer, forming a long, sausage-like shape. Repeat with the remaining mixture and skewers.
6. Lightly oil the grill grates to prevent sticking. Place the skewers of meat onto the grill and cook for 5-6 minutes per side, or until the kebabs are cooked through and have nice grill marks.
7. Once cooked, remove the kebabs from the grill and let them rest for a few minutes before serving.
8. While the kebabs are cooking, prepare the yogurt sauce. In a small bowl, combine the Greek yogurt, minced garlic, dried mint, salt, and pepper. Mix well and set aside.
9. In a skillet, heat olive oil over medium heat. Add the finely chopped onion and sauté until translucent.
10. Add the chopped spinach to the skillet and cook until wilted. Season with salt and pepper to taste.
11. To serve, place the cooked spinach on a serving platter. Top with the grilled kebabs and drizzle with the yogurt sauce.
12. Serve the Kebab-e Borani hot with rice, bread, or salad.

Enjoy your delicious and flavorful Borani Kebab!

Kebab-e Dandeh (Sheep Kebab)

Ingredients:

- 1.5 pounds sheep meat (such as lamb or mutton), cut into cubes
- 1 onion, grated
- 2 cloves garlic, minced
- Juice of 1 lemon
- 2 tablespoons plain yogurt
- 2 tablespoons olive oil
- 1 teaspoon ground turmeric
- 1 teaspoon ground cumin
- 1 teaspoon ground coriander
- 1 teaspoon ground black pepper
- 1 teaspoon salt, or to taste
- Wooden skewers, soaked in water for at least 30 minutes

Instructions:

1. In a mixing bowl, combine the grated onion, minced garlic, lemon juice, yogurt, olive oil, ground turmeric, cumin, coriander, black pepper, and salt. Mix well to form a marinade.
2. Add the cubed sheep meat to the marinade mixture and toss until all the pieces are evenly coated. Cover the bowl with plastic wrap and refrigerate for at least 2 hours, or overnight for best results, to allow the flavors to meld.
3. Preheat your grill to medium-high heat. If using charcoal, wait until the coals are ashed over.
4. Thread the marinated meat onto the soaked wooden skewers, making sure they are evenly distributed.
5. Lightly oil the grill grates to prevent sticking. Place the skewers of meat onto the grill and cook for about 6-8 minutes per side, or until the meat is cooked through and has nice grill marks.
6. Once cooked, remove the kebabs from the grill and let them rest for a few minutes before serving.
7. Serve the Kebab-e Dandeh hot with rice, bread, grilled vegetables, or salad.

Enjoy the delicious and flavorful taste of Sheep Kebab, a classic Persian dish!

Kebab-e Shalgham

Ingredients:

- 1 pound lamb or beef, cut into cubes
- 4 medium-sized turnips, peeled and cut into thick slices
- 1 onion, finely chopped
- 2 cloves garlic, minced
- 2 tablespoons olive oil
- Juice of 1 lemon
- 1 teaspoon ground turmeric
- 1 teaspoon ground cumin
- 1 teaspoon ground coriander
- 1 teaspoon paprika
- Salt and pepper to taste
- Wooden skewers, soaked in water for at least 30 minutes

Instructions:

1. In a bowl, combine the chopped onion, minced garlic, olive oil, lemon juice, turmeric, cumin, coriander, paprika, salt, and pepper. Mix well to form a marinade.
2. Add the cubed meat to the marinade and toss until evenly coated. Cover the bowl and refrigerate for at least 2 hours, or overnight for best results, to allow the flavors to meld.
3. Preheat your grill to medium-high heat. If using charcoal, wait until the coals are ashed over.
4. Thread the marinated meat onto the soaked wooden skewers, alternating with the slices of turnip.
5. Lightly oil the grill grates to prevent sticking. Place the skewers on the grill and cook for about 10-12 minutes, turning occasionally, or until the meat is cooked through and the turnips are tender.
6. Once cooked, remove the kebabs from the grill and let them rest for a few minutes before serving.
7. Serve the Kebab-e Shalgham hot with rice, bread, or salad.

Enjoy the unique and delicious flavor of Turnip Kebab, a delightful dish that's sure to impress!

Kebab-e Jigar (Liver Kebab)

Ingredients:

- 1 pound beef or lamb liver, sliced into thin strips
- 1 onion, finely chopped
- 2 cloves garlic, minced
- 2 tablespoons plain yogurt
- Juice of 1 lemon
- 2 tablespoons olive oil
- 1 teaspoon ground turmeric
- 1 teaspoon ground cumin
- 1 teaspoon ground coriander
- 1 teaspoon paprika
- Salt and pepper to taste
- Wooden skewers, soaked in water for at least 30 minutes

Instructions:

1. In a mixing bowl, combine the chopped onion, minced garlic, plain yogurt, lemon juice, olive oil, ground turmeric, cumin, coriander, paprika, salt, and pepper. Mix well to form a marinade.
2. Add the sliced liver to the marinade mixture and toss until all pieces are evenly coated. Cover the bowl with plastic wrap and refrigerate for at least 2 hours, allowing the flavors to meld.
3. Preheat your grill to medium-high heat. If using charcoal, wait until the coals are ashed over.
4. Thread the marinated liver slices onto the soaked wooden skewers.
5. Lightly oil the grill grates to prevent sticking. Place the skewers on the grill and cook for about 3-4 minutes per side, or until the liver is cooked through and has a nice char.
6. Once cooked, remove the kebabs from the grill and let them rest for a few minutes.
7. Serve the Kebab-e Jigar hot with rice, bread, or salad.

Enjoy the rich and flavorful taste of Liver Kebab, a classic dish loved by many!

Kebab-e Falafel (Falafel Kebab)

Ingredients:

For the falafel:

- 2 cups cooked chickpeas (canned or cooked from dried)
- 1 small onion, finely chopped
- 3 cloves garlic, minced
- 1/4 cup fresh parsley, chopped
- 1/4 cup fresh cilantro, chopped
- 1 teaspoon ground cumin
- 1 teaspoon ground coriander
- 1/2 teaspoon baking soda
- 2 tablespoons all-purpose flour or chickpea flour (besan)
- Salt and pepper to taste
- Vegetable oil for frying

For assembling the kebabs:

- Pita bread or flatbread
- Lettuce, tomatoes, cucumbers, and any other desired toppings
- Tahini sauce or tzatziki sauce for serving

Instructions:

1. In a food processor, combine the cooked chickpeas, chopped onion, minced garlic, chopped parsley, chopped cilantro, ground cumin, ground coriander, baking soda, flour, salt, and pepper. Pulse until the mixture forms a coarse paste.
2. Transfer the falafel mixture to a bowl and refrigerate for at least 30 minutes to firm up.
3. Once the falafel mixture has chilled, shape it into small patties or balls, about 1-2 inches in diameter.
4. Heat vegetable oil in a skillet or deep fryer to 350°F (175°C). Carefully place the falafel patties or balls into the hot oil and fry until golden brown and crispy, about 3-4 minutes per side. Work in batches to avoid overcrowding the skillet or fryer.
5. Once the falafel is cooked, transfer it to a plate lined with paper towels to drain any excess oil.

6. To assemble the kebabs, warm the pita bread or flatbread. Place a few falafel patties or balls on each piece of bread, along with lettuce, tomatoes, cucumbers, and any other desired toppings.
7. Drizzle tahini sauce or tzatziki sauce over the falafel and toppings.
8. Roll up the pita bread or flatbread to enclose the filling and serve immediately.

Enjoy your homemade Kebab-e Falafel, a delicious fusion of flavors that's perfect for any occasion!

Kebab-e Khashkhash (Poppy Seed Kebab)

Ingredients:

For the kebabs:

- 1 pound ground beef or lamb
- 1 onion, finely chopped
- 2 cloves garlic, minced
- 2 tablespoons poppy seeds
- 2 tablespoons plain yogurt
- Juice of 1 lemon
- 2 tablespoons olive oil
- 1 teaspoon ground cumin
- 1 teaspoon ground coriander
- 1 teaspoon paprika
- Salt and pepper to taste
- Wooden skewers, soaked in water for at least 30 minutes

For the garnish:

- Chopped fresh parsley or cilantro
- Lemon wedges

Instructions:

1. In a bowl, combine the ground meat, chopped onion, minced garlic, poppy seeds, plain yogurt, lemon juice, olive oil, ground cumin, ground coriander, paprika, salt, and pepper. Mix well until all ingredients are evenly incorporated.
2. Cover the bowl and refrigerate the mixture for at least 1 hour to allow the flavors to meld.
3. Preheat your grill to medium-high heat. If using charcoal, wait until the coals are ashed over.
4. Take the skewers and divide the meat mixture evenly among them, shaping the meat around the skewers to form kebabs.

5. Lightly oil the grill grates to prevent sticking. Place the skewers on the grill and cook for about 4-5 minutes on each side, or until the kebabs are cooked through and have nice grill marks.
6. Once cooked, remove the kebabs from the grill and let them rest for a few minutes.
7. Serve the Kebab-e Khashkhash hot, garnished with chopped fresh parsley or cilantro, and lemon wedges on the side.

Enjoy the unique and flavorful taste of Poppy Seed Kebab, a delightful dish that's sure to impress!

Kebab-e Mast (Yogurt Kebab)

Ingredients:

For the kebabs:

- 1 pound boneless lamb or beef, cut into cubes
- 1 onion, grated
- 2 cloves garlic, minced
- 1 cup plain yogurt
- Juice of 1 lemon
- 2 tablespoons olive oil
- 1 teaspoon ground turmeric
- 1 teaspoon ground cumin
- 1 teaspoon ground coriander
- 1 teaspoon paprika
- Salt and pepper to taste
- Wooden skewers, soaked in water for at least 30 minutes

For the yogurt sauce:

- 1 cup plain yogurt
- 2 tablespoons chopped fresh mint
- 2 tablespoons chopped fresh parsley
- 2 tablespoons chopped fresh cilantro
- Salt and pepper to taste

Instructions:

1. In a bowl, combine the grated onion, minced garlic, plain yogurt, lemon juice, olive oil, ground turmeric, ground cumin, ground coriander, paprika, salt, and pepper. Mix well to form a marinade.
2. Add the cubed meat to the marinade and toss until evenly coated. Cover the bowl and refrigerate for at least 2 hours, or overnight for best results, to allow the flavors to meld.
3. Preheat your grill to medium-high heat. If using charcoal, wait until the coals are ashed over.

4. Thread the marinated meat onto the soaked wooden skewers.
5. Lightly oil the grill grates to prevent sticking. Place the skewers on the grill and cook for about 10-12 minutes, turning occasionally, or until the meat is cooked through and has nice grill marks.
6. While the kebabs are cooking, prepare the yogurt sauce. In a small bowl, combine the plain yogurt, chopped fresh mint, parsley, cilantro, salt, and pepper. Mix well.
7. Once the kebabs are cooked, remove them from the grill and let them rest for a few minutes.
8. Serve the Kebab-e Mast hot with the yogurt sauce on the side for dipping.

Enjoy the tender and flavorful taste of Yogurt Kebab, a delightful dish that's perfect for any occasion!

Kebab-e Jujeh (Cornish Hen Kebab)

Ingredients:

- 2 Cornish hens, each cut into pieces (or you can use chicken pieces)
- 1 onion, grated
- 3 cloves garlic, minced
- Juice of 2 lemons
- 1/2 cup plain yogurt
- 1/4 cup olive oil
- 1 teaspoon ground saffron threads (dissolved in 2 tablespoons hot water)
- 1 teaspoon ground turmeric
- 1 teaspoon ground cumin
- 1 teaspoon ground coriander
- Salt and pepper to taste
- Wooden skewers, soaked in water for at least 30 minutes

Instructions:

1. In a large bowl, combine the grated onion, minced garlic, lemon juice, plain yogurt, olive oil, dissolved saffron, ground turmeric, ground cumin, ground coriander, salt, and pepper. Mix well to form a marinade.
2. Add the Cornish hen pieces to the marinade and toss until evenly coated. Cover the bowl and refrigerate for at least 4 hours, or overnight for best results, to allow the flavors to meld.
3. Preheat your grill to medium-high heat. If using charcoal, wait until the coals are ashed over.
4. Thread the marinated Cornish hen pieces onto the soaked wooden skewers.
5. Lightly oil the grill grates to prevent sticking. Place the skewers on the grill and cook for about 20-25 minutes, turning occasionally, or until the Cornish hen is cooked through and has nice grill marks.
6. Once cooked, remove the kebabs from the grill and let them rest for a few minutes.
7. Serve the Kebab-e Jujeh hot with rice, bread, or salad.

Enjoy the delicious and aromatic flavor of Cornish Hen Kebab, a classic Persian dish that's sure to impress!

Kebab-e Sabzi (Herb Kebab)

Ingredients:

- 1 pound ground beef or lamb
- 1 cup chopped fresh parsley
- 1 cup chopped fresh cilantro
- 1 cup chopped fresh dill
- 1 cup chopped green onions (both green and white parts)
- 1 onion, grated
- 3 cloves garlic, minced
- 2 tablespoons ground walnuts (optional)
- 2 tablespoons dried fenugreek leaves (optional)
- 1 teaspoon ground turmeric
- 1 teaspoon ground cumin
- 1 teaspoon ground coriander
- Salt and pepper to taste
- Wooden skewers, soaked in water for at least 30 minutes

Instructions:

1. In a large mixing bowl, combine the ground meat, chopped fresh herbs (parsley, cilantro, dill, and green onions), grated onion, minced garlic, ground walnuts, dried fenugreek leaves (if using), ground turmeric, ground cumin, ground coriander, salt, and pepper. Mix well until all ingredients are evenly distributed.
2. Cover the bowl and refrigerate the mixture for at least 1 hour to allow the flavors to meld.
3. Preheat your grill to medium-high heat. If using charcoal, wait until the coals are ashed over.
4. Take the soaked wooden skewers and divide the meat mixture evenly among them, shaping the meat around the skewers to form kebabs.
5. Lightly oil the grill grates to prevent sticking. Place the skewers on the grill and cook for about 10-12 minutes, turning occasionally, or until the kebabs are cooked through and have nice grill marks.
6. Once cooked, remove the kebabs from the grill and let them rest for a few minutes.
7. Serve the Kebab-e Sabzi hot with rice, bread, or salad.

Enjoy the delicious and aromatic flavor of Herb Kebab, a delightful Persian dish that's perfect for any occasion!

Kebab-e Taze (Fresh Kebab)

Ingredients:

- 1 pound ground lamb or beef
- 1 onion, finely chopped
- 3 cloves garlic, minced
- 1/2 cup chopped fresh mint leaves
- 1/2 cup chopped fresh parsley
- 1/2 cup chopped fresh cilantro
- 2 tablespoons chopped fresh dill
- 1 tablespoon ground sumac
- 1 tablespoon ground cumin
- 1 tablespoon ground coriander
- 1 teaspoon paprika
- Juice of 1 lemon
- Salt and pepper to taste
- Wooden skewers, soaked in water for at least 30 minutes

Instructions:

1. In a large mixing bowl, combine the ground meat, chopped onion, minced garlic, chopped fresh herbs (mint, parsley, cilantro, and dill), ground sumac, ground cumin, ground coriander, paprika, lemon juice, salt, and pepper. Mix well until all ingredients are evenly distributed.
2. Cover the bowl and refrigerate the mixture for at least 30 minutes to allow the flavors to meld.
3. Preheat your grill to medium-high heat. If using charcoal, wait until the coals are ashed over.
4. Take the soaked wooden skewers and divide the meat mixture evenly among them, shaping the meat around the skewers to form kebabs.
5. Lightly oil the grill grates to prevent sticking. Place the skewers on the grill and cook for about 8-10 minutes, turning occasionally, or until the kebabs are cooked through and have nice grill marks.
6. Once cooked, remove the kebabs from the grill and let them rest for a few minutes.
7. Serve the Kebab-e Taze hot with rice, bread, or salad.

Enjoy the fresh and flavorful taste of Fresh Kebab, a delightful Persian dish that's perfect for any occasion!

Kebab-e Shirazi (Shirazi Kebab)

Ingredients:

- 2 medium cucumbers, diced
- 2 medium tomatoes, diced
- 1 small red onion, finely chopped
- 1/4 cup chopped fresh parsley
- 1/4 cup chopped fresh mint
- Juice of 1-2 lemons, to taste
- 2 tablespoons extra virgin olive oil
- Salt and pepper to taste

Instructions:

1. In a large mixing bowl, combine the diced cucumbers, tomatoes, chopped red onion, chopped parsley, and chopped mint.
2. Drizzle the lemon juice and olive oil over the salad.
3. Season with salt and pepper, to taste.
4. Toss the salad gently until all ingredients are well combined and evenly coated with the dressing.
5. Cover the bowl and refrigerate the salad for at least 30 minutes to allow the flavors to meld.
6. Serve the Shirazi salad chilled as a refreshing side dish to your kebab platter.

For the kebab platter, you can choose your favorite kebab recipes from the ones mentioned earlier and serve them alongside the Shirazi salad. Enjoy your delicious Persian-inspired meal!

Kebab-e Esfenaj (Spinach Kebab)

Ingredients:

- 2 cups fresh spinach, finely chopped
- 1 cup cooked green lentils
- 1 small onion, finely chopped
- 2 cloves garlic, minced
- 1/4 cup fresh parsley, chopped
- 1/4 cup fresh cilantro, chopped
- 2 tablespoons fresh mint, chopped
- 1 teaspoon ground turmeric
- 1 teaspoon ground cumin
- 1 teaspoon ground sumac (optional)
- Salt and pepper to taste
- Olive oil for frying

Instructions:

1. In a large mixing bowl, combine the finely chopped spinach, cooked lentils, chopped onion, minced garlic, chopped parsley, cilantro, and mint.
2. Add the ground turmeric, ground cumin, ground sumac (if using), salt, and pepper to the bowl. Mix everything together until well combined.
3. Using your hands, shape the mixture into small patties or form them onto skewers.
4. Heat a little olive oil in a skillet or grill pan over medium heat.
5. Once the oil is hot, add the spinach kebabs to the skillet in batches, making sure not to overcrowd the pan.
6. Cook the kebabs for about 3-4 minutes on each side, or until they are golden brown and crispy on the outside.
7. Once cooked, remove the kebabs from the skillet and place them on a plate lined with paper towels to drain any excess oil.
8. Serve the Spinach Kebabs hot with your favorite dipping sauce, yogurt sauce, or alongside a fresh salad and warm flatbread.

Enjoy your delicious and nutritious Spinach Kebabs!

www.ingramcontent.com/pod-product-compliance
Lightning Source LLC
LaVergne TN
LVHW081612060526
838201LV00054B/2215